Questions and Answers: Countries

Argentina

A Question and Answer Book

by Mary Englar

Consultant:
Colin M. MacLachlan
John Christy Barr Distinguished Professor of History
Tulane University
New Orleans, Louisiana

Mankato, Minnesota

Fact Finders is published by Capstone Press,
151 Good Counsel Drive, P.O. Box 669, Mankato, Minnesota 56002.
www.capstonepress.com

Copyright © 2006 by Capstone Press. All rights reserved.
No part of this publication may be reproduced in whole or in part, or stored in a retrieval system, or transmitted in any form or by any means, electronic, mechanical, photocopying, recording, or otherwise, without written permission of the publisher.
For information regarding permission, write to Capstone Press,
151 Good Counsel Drive, P.O. Box 669, Dept. R, Mankato, Minnesota 56002.
Printed in the United States of America

Library of Congress Cataloging-in-Publication Data
Englar, Mary.
    Argentina : a question and answer book / by Mary Englar.
    p. cm. —(Fact finders. Questions and answers. Countries)
    Summary: "Describes the geography, history, economy, and culture of Argentina in a question-and-answer format"–Provided by publisher.
    Includes bibliographical references and index.
    ISBN 0–7368–4350–7 (hardcover)
    1. Argentina—Juvenile literature. I. Title. II. Series.
F2808.2.E54 2006
982—dc22   2005001159

Editorial Credits
Silver Editions, editorial, design, and production; Kia Adams, set designer; Ortelius Design, Inc., cartographer; Wanda Winch, photo researcher; Scott Thoms, photo editor

Photo Credits
Corbis/Owen Franken, 19; Reuters, 9; Royalty-Free, 1
Cory Langley, cover (foreground), 27
Craig Lovell, cover (background)
Houserstock/Michael J. Pettypool, 25
One Mile Up, Inc., 29 (flag)
Photo Courtesy of Paul Baker, 29 (coins)
Photo Courtesy of Richard Sutherland, 29 (bill)
South American Pictures/Chris Sharp, 17; Frank Nowikowski, 22–23; Kathy Jarvis, 21; Marion Morrison, 7; Sue Mann, 15; Tony Morrison, 4, 11, 12–13

Artistic Effects:
Photodisc/Jules Frazier, 18

1 2 3 4 5 6 10 09 08 07 06 05

Table of Contents

Where is Argentina? 4
When did Argentina become a country? 6
What type of government does Argentina have? 8
What kind of housing does Argentina have? 10
What are Argentina's forms of transportation? 12
What are Argentina's major industries? 14
What is school like in Argentina? 16
What are Argentina's favorite sports and games? 18
What are the traditional art forms in Argentina? 20
What major holidays do Argentines celebrate? 22
What are the traditional foods of Argentina? 24
What is family life like in Argentina? 26

Features

Argentina Fast Facts 28
Money and Flag 29
Learn to Speak Spanish 30
Glossary 30
Internet Sites 31
Read More 31
Index 32

Where is Argentina?

Argentina is a large country in South America. It is four times bigger than Texas. Argentina is closer to Antarctica than any other country in the world.

The Andes Mountains form much of the country's western border. Mount Aconcagua is 22,831 feet (6,959 meters) high. It is the tallest mountain in the Americas.

Ranchers raise cattle in the flat grasslands of the Pampas.

Grasslands cover most of central Argentina. These flat plains, called the **Pampas**, have few trees. Cattle graze on the grasses.

When did Argentina become a country?

Argentina became a country in 1816. Before that, it was a **colony** of Spain. The Spanish explored Argentina in the 1500s. They were looking for silver and gold.

The Spanish first settled in the north. Later, they started cattle ranches on the Pampas. The ranchers hired cowboys, who were called **gauchos**. Many gauchos were American Indians who lived on the Pampas.

Fact!

In 1993, scientists discovered the bones of a new dinosaur in Argentina. The giganotosaurus is the largest meat-eater ever found.

This statue honors José de San Martín, a hero in Argentina's fight for independence.

By the early 1800s, Argentines wanted to be independent. In 1810, they set up their own government. José de San Martín led the fight against the Spanish. For six years, they fought the Spanish. In 1816, Argentina declared independence from Spain.

What type of government does Argentina have?

Argentina is a **republic**. The Argentine people vote for their leaders. All Argentines age 18 and older can vote.

The Argentine government is similar to the U.S. government. The people vote for a president and a vice president. The president is the head of the government. He or she is also the head of the army.

Fact!

The presidential palace is called the Casa Rosada. This means "Pink House" in Spanish. The palace was painted pink when it was converted from a post office to the presidential palace.

The National Congress meets to discuss new laws.

Argentina has a National Congress. The Congress makes the country's laws. It has a Senate and a Chamber of Deputies. The National Congress meets in Buenos Aires, the capital city.

What kind of housing does Argentina have?

Argentines live in apartments and houses. In Buenos Aires, most people live in apartments. The city is very crowded.

Many Argentines look for work in Buenos Aires. Some do not have enough money to rent apartments. Instead, they build houses out of old wood and tin.

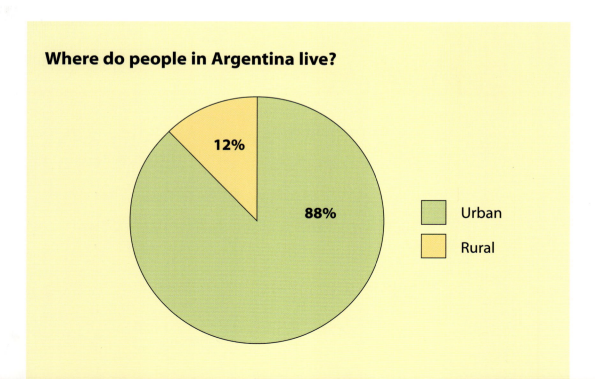

Where do people in Argentina live?

12%
88%
Urban
Rural

Both poor neighborhoods and tall, modern buildings can be seen in Buenos Aires.

In rural areas, most Argentines live in homes made of **adobe**. These homes have dirt floors and roofs of straw and mud.

Some wealthy Argentines own large homes on rural ranches. These ranches can be far from towns. They have their own schools and airports.

What are Argentina's forms of transportation?

Argentina has many forms of transportation. Cars, trucks, taxis, and buses fill the streets in Buenos Aires. Trains run from downtown to the **suburbs**.

The subway in Buenos Aires opened in 1913. It is the oldest subway in South America. Most of the subway cars are new, but some old wooden cars still run.

Fact!

Northern Argentina has one of the highest railroads in the world. The Train to the Clouds climbs up the Andes Mountains. At the top, travelers are 13,850 feet (4,197 meters) above sea level.

Argentines take buses, taxis, or walk to get around Buenos Aires.

Argentina is a very large country. Most people travel by bus or train between cities. Many people ride airplanes when they have to travel long distances within the country.

What are Argentina's major industries?

Agriculture and ranching are Argentina's most important industries. Farmers grow cotton, soybeans, sugarcane, and wheat. Ranchers raise cattle and sheep. Cattle provide meat and leather. Sheep provide meat and wool.

Argentina also has many factories. Some pack and ship beef to other countries. Other factories turn cowhides into leather. The steel industry produces metal for Argentina's car factories.

What does Argentina import and export?	
Imports	**Exports**
chemicals	beef
equipment	grain
machinery	natural gas

Ranchers round up sheep on a large ranch on the Pampas.

Argentina has many natural resources. Oil and natural gas supply most of the country's energy needs. In 1997, a new copper and gold mine opened in the northwest Andes Mountains.

What is school like in Argentina?

School is free for Argentine children from grade school through college. Children between the ages of 6 and 14 must go to school. The school year lasts from March until December.

Some parents send their children to private schools. Many private schools teach students in two languages. Students learn in Spanish. They also learn in English or French.

Fact!

In their last year of high school, Argentine students celebrate with a class trip. This special trip is called the Viajes de Egresados, or the "leaving school trip."

Students in a private school classroom raise their hands to answer a question.

Students must buy their own books and supplies. For some children, books and supplies cost too much. They cannot finish school. They must go to work to help their families.

What are Argentina's favorite sports and games?

Soccer is called *fútbol* in Spanish. It is Argentina's favorite sport. Boys often get soccer balls for their first birthday. The Boca Juniors and the River Plate are two popular soccer teams. Fans light firecrackers at games when their favorite team scores.

The Argentine National Team has become one of the best in the world. They won the gold medal in the 2004 Olympics.

Fact!

Manu Ginobili is a basketball star for the San Antonio Spurs. He played on the Argentine basketball team in the 2004 Olympics. The team won the gold medal.

Argentines enjoy playing a game of pato.

Argentines love horses and are good riders. Polo and horse racing are popular. One game on horseback is called *pato*. *Pato* means duck. In the past, players put a live duck in a leather basket. Today, *pato* players use a leather ball.

What are the traditional art forms in Argentina?

Music and dancing are part of every celebration in Argentina. The tango is the most famous dance of Argentina. The tango has slow, difficult steps. The music often sounds sad. The orchestra includes a violin, a piano, and an accordion.

Fact!

The Cave of Hands is located in the Province of Santa Cruz in southern Argentina. It was painted almost 10,000 years ago. There are outlines of hundreds of hands on the cave walls.

Dancers perform the tango in an outdoor square in Buenos Aires.

Many famous artists have come from Argentina. In the 1920s, Florencio Molina Campos drew pictures of Argentine life. He became famous for his drawings of gauchos and their horses.

What major holidays do Argentines celebrate?

Argentines celebrate many Roman Catholic holidays. Christmas is an important family holiday. In South America, the seasons are the opposite of the United States. Christmas is in the middle of summer. Families get together to eat, sing, and dance. At midnight, they watch fireworks.

Another important celebration is Carnival. This comes about six weeks before Easter. People dress in costumes and dance.

What other holidays do people in Argentina celebrate?

Independence Day
Labor Day
New Year's Day

In Buenos Aires, Argentines celebrate Christmas with lots of fireworks.

Many towns also have **festivals**. In November, the Day of Tradition honors gauchos. Gauchos ride their best horses in festival parades. They also ride wild horses in rodeos.

What are the traditional foods of Argentina?

Most Argentine meals include beef. Stew, sausages, and steak are popular. Argentines eat most parts of the cow. Steakhouses serve beef with heart, liver, tongue, and brain.

Many Italians moved to Argentina in the 1800s. They brought their favorite foods with them. Spaghetti, lasagna, and pizza are all popular in Argentina today.

Fact!

Every year, Argentines eat more than 130 pounds (59 kilograms) of beef per person.

On large ranches, meals sometimes include barbecued meat.

Sweets and ice cream are also popular. A creamy caramel called *dulce de leche* is used in many desserts. Ice cream shops sell more than 50 kinds of ice cream.

What is family life like in Argentina?

Argentine families like to live near their relatives. Families are very close. Older children live at home until they get married.

In the past, fathers worked and mothers stayed home. Now, almost half of Argentine women work outside the home.

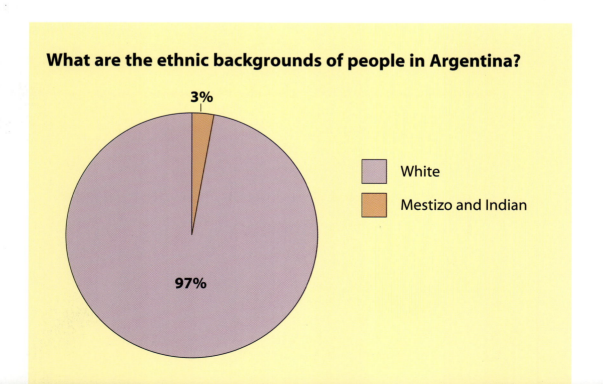

What are the ethnic backgrounds of people in Argentina?

3%

97%

White

Mestizo and Indian

Argentine families often get together to share a meal.

Argentina is a nation of **immigrants**. People have come from Spain, Italy, and other countries. Families follow some old traditions. But all families see themselves as Argentines.

Argentina Fast Facts

Official name:
Argentine Republic

Land area:
1,067,309 square miles
(2,736,690 square kilometers)

Average annual precipitation:
40 inches (102 centimeters)

Average January temperature (Buenos Aires):
74 degrees Fahrenheit
(23 degrees Celsius)

Average July temperature (Buenos Aires):
50 degrees Fahrenheit
(10 degrees Celsius)

Population:
39,144,753 people

Capital city:
Buenos Aires

Language:
Spanish

Natural resources:
copper, iron ore, lead, manganese, oil, tin, uranium, zinc

Religions:

Roman Catholic	92%
Protestant	2%
Jewish	2%
Other	4%

Money and Flag

Money:

Argentina's money is the peso. In 2005, one U.S. dollar equaled 2.91 pesos. One Canadian dollar equaled 2.36 pesos.

Flag:

The Argentine flag has three stripes. Blue represents the sky, and white stands for clouds. The bright yellow sun is called the Sun of May.

Learn to Speak Spanish

Most people in Argentina speak Spanish. It is Argentina's official language. Learn to speak some Spanish words using the chart below.

English	Spanish	Pronunciation
good morning	buenos días	(BWAY-nohs DEE-ahs)
good-bye	adiós	(ah-dee-OHS)
please	por favor	(POR fah-VOR)
thank you	gracias	(GRAH-see-us)
yes	sí	(SEE)
no	no	(NOH)
How are you?	¿Cómo estás?	(KOH-moh ay-STAHS)
I'm fine	bien	(BEE-en)

Glossary

adobe (uh-DOH-bee)—clay mixed with water and straw

colony (KOL-uh-nee)—an area that is settled by people from another country and that is ruled by that country

gauchos (GOW-chohs)—cowboys of the South American grassland

festival (FESS-tuh-vuhl)—a celebration

immigrant (IM-uh-gruhnt)—a person who comes to live permanently in a country

Pampas (PAM-puhz)— an area of large grasslands in Argentina

republic (ree-PUHB-lik)—a government headed by a president with officials elected by the people

suburb (SUHB-urb)—a town near the edge of a city

Internet Sites

FactHound offers a safe, fun way to find Internet sites related to this book. All of the sites on FactHound have been researched by our staff.

Here's how:
1. Visit *www.facthound.com*
2. Type in this special code **0736843507** for age-appropriate sites. Or enter a search word related to this book for a more general search.
3. Click on the **Fetch It** button.

FactHound will fetch the best sites for you!

Read More

Conley, Kate A. *Argentina.* The Countries. Edina, Minn.: Abdo, 2004.

Fearns, Les and Daisy. *Argentina.* Countries of the World. New York: Facts on File, Inc., 2005.

Gordon, Sharon. *Argentina.* Discovering Cultures. New York: Benchmark Books, 2003.

Lourie, Peter. *Tierra del Fuego: A Journey to the End of the Earth.* Honesdale, Pa.: Boyds Mills Press, 2002.

Index

agriculture, 4, 6, 14
Andes Mountains, 4, 12, 15
art forms, 20–21

Buenos Aires, 9, 10, 11, 12, 13, 21, 23, 28

Campos, Florencio Molina, 21
capital. See Buenos Aires
Casa Rosada, 8
climate, 22, 28

education, 11, 16–17
ethnic groups, 26
exports, 14

families, 17, 26–27
farming. See agriculture
flag, 29
food, 24–25

games, 18–19
gauchos, 6, 21, 23
giganotosaurus, 6
Ginobili, Manu, 18
government, 8–9

holidays, 22–23
housing, 10–11

immigrants, 24, 27
imports, 14
independence, 7
industries, 14–15

landforms, 4–5
language, 16, 28, 30

money, 29
Mount Aconcagua, 4

National Congress, 9
natural resources, 6, 15, 28

Pampas, 4, 6, 15
population, 10, 28

ranches, 6, 11, 14, 15
religion, 22, 28

San Martín, José de, 7
schools. See education
Spain, 6, 7
sports, 18–19

tango, 20, 21
transportation, 12–13

weather. See climate

1740